Monteverdi Madrigals

Denis Arnold

£3-50

AD

DENIS ARNOLD

MONTEVERDI
Madrigals

BBC MUSIC GUIDES

ARIEL MUSIC
BBC BOOKS

Published by BBC Books
A division of BBC Enterprises Ltd
80 Wood Lane, London W12 0TT

ISBN 0 563 20555 5

First published 1967
Reprinted 1975, 1978
First published in Ariel Music 1987

Typeset in 10/11 pt Garamond by Phoenix Photosetting, Chatham
Printed in England by Mackays of Chatham Ltd

Contents

The Madrigal

. . . But supper being ended and music books (according to the custom) being brought to the table, the mistress of the house presented me with a part earnestly requesting me to sing; but when, with many excuses, I protested unfeignedly that I could not, everyone began to wonder; yea some whispered to others demanding how I was brought up, so that upon shame of mine ignorance I go now to seek out mine old friend Master Gnorimus, to make myself his scholar . . .[1]

Morley's description of a madrigalian evening is, of course, charming; it is also somewhat misleading. Its suggestion of the Elizabethan dilettante's delight in music-making may make us believe that the madrigal and its associated genres, the canzonet and ballett, were predominantly music for the amateur. On the contrary, there is ample evidence that, in Italy at least, these forms were the delight of the professional performer, and their audience. There is also more than a hint by Morley that the madrigal was essentially chamber music, written for a quartet or quintet of singers. Again this is something of an oversimplification, for we know that they were sometimes performed by choirs, and more often still by a mixed ensemble of singers and instrumentalists. Most of all, Morley seems (perhaps not by design) to suggest that such music is to be limited by the understanding and techniques of the genteman, the ideal courtier of Castiglione's *Il Libro del Cortegiano* or Sir Thomas Elyot's *Governour*.

This may not be too unjust to some of the minor English composers of the era. It certainly gives the wrong impression of the great Italians. Marenzio, Monteverdi, and Marco da Gagliano (to mention no others) are among the finest composers of the age and, it may be said, of all time. They chose to compose madrigals because the genre offered them a vehicle for expressing their profounder feelings. It seemed no more a pleasant miniature to them than song seemed to Schubert, Wolf or Brahms. Perhaps, indeed, the best approach to the madrigal is through song, for the two present many of the same problems to the composer, and both have many of the same potentialities and limitations. Both rely on finding a suitable kind of poetry, not too abstract, but suggestive of emotional power. Both make the composer find a musical imagery which will match that of the verse. Both at their best have an unmatched

1 *A Plain and Easy Introduction to Practical Music*, ed. Alec Harman (London, 1952), p. 9.

intensity which seems to have a more immediate effect on man than any comparable musical form.

Many of the considerations which we must apply to the composers of *Lieder* apply to Monteverdi. His collected madrigalian output shows the fluctuations we find in the song books of the nineteenth-century masters. The type of verse which was popular at various times throughout his long life is reflected in his madrigal books. When it was frivolous or at least not very intense, his music matches its superficiality. When it becomes mannerist and exaggerated (more particularly in the verse of Guarini and Marini) the mood of the music becomes exaggerated too. When the fashion was for strong, concrete imagery, the music follows its pictorialism; when the vogue was for more abstract, philosophical verse, so does Monteverdi's music become more abstract. And when he met various poets, as he most certainly did Tasso and Guarini, the accessibility of their verse naturally tempted him to set it to music.

Performers, too, quite clearly helped to shape his style. Just as if Schubert had never met the court singer Vogl his songs would surely have never acquired the sublety which this singer could bring to them, so it is inconceivable that the florid upper parts of Monteverdi's middle-period madrigals would have develope d their expressive virtuoso qualities if it had not been for the splendidly agile throats of the Mantuan prima donnas. Nor should we have had the magnificent tenor duets and bass solos of his Venetian music if it had not been for his colleagues in the strictly masculine choir of St Mark's, which had in it such friends as Giovanni Battista Marinoni and Giacomo Rapallini, whose praises he so often sang in his letters to the Mantuan court. Was it for the famed castrati of this choir that he wrote such works as 'Se i languidi miei sguardi' and perhaps 'Chiome d'oro', which set verse more suitable for male than female sopranos? And even if it was not the Venetian taste for eunuchs which directly inspired these works, the instrumental ensembles required by Monteverdi without doubt came from the forces to hand. The dozen instruments required by 'Con che soavità' were all to be found in the orchestra of St Mark's, just as the ensemble for which the ballet *Tirsi e Clori* was written was specifically designed with the resources of Mantua in mind. Monteverdi was a thoroughly professional composer.

He was also very human, and if the external circumstances of his life shaped the manner of his music, it was his inner life which so often is reflected in its matter. No doubt like any good dramatist, Monteverdi was capable of imagining the state of mind of the lovers of his favoured pastoral poets. It would certainly be dangerous to assume that every madrigal is a personal document. But equally there is little doubt that his madrigal books do reveal a great deal of the man. Only someone who had suffered a great personal loss could have so vividly portrayed the loneliness in the laments of his *Sixth Book of Madrigals* or the 'Lament of the Nymph' of the *Eighth Book*. Only someone who had seen warfare at first hand could have composed his *madrigali guerrieri*. As certain images recur in his madrigalian verse, and certain musical attitudes to these images are repeated, we begin to realise how self-revealing the process of setting words to music is, especially when the composer has more or less complete power of selection of his poetry, as Monteverdi had in his madrigals.

Charm at Cremona

MADRIGALI SPIRITUALI (1583); CANZONETTE (1584); BOOKS I AND II OF
MADRIGALI A 5 VOCI (1587 AND 1590)

Monteverdi started as a composer of charm. After all, this is the best
that a boy of sixteen can hope for. And charm was highly prized in the
music of the 1580s. The heroic age of the madrigal seemingly was past.
The battles fought by the old Netherlanders such as Willaert and
Cipriano de Rore, to make secular music as powerful and expressive as
music for the church, were over and won. The settings of classical poets
were full of high seriousness and moral purpose. They were admired –
but not imitated. The composers of the moment were those for whom
the madrigal was the expression of lighter moods. Their love affairs were
the not-too-serious flirtations of the shepherds and shepherdesses of the
latest pastoral verse, not of the self-renouncing Petrarch whose beloved
was worshipped from afar. At worst the pastoral lovers would suffer the
delightful delays of courtship; at best they could hope for the joys of a
consummated union. Their sadness calls for music with a gentle pathos,
with perhaps some mild dissonance (but, to quote the best known
theorist of the time, 'never so severe as to offend'[1], and even an
occasional chromatic harmony. Their joys are best conveyed by memorable, easily sung rhythms, and the bright colours of the upper voices
and the major key. Andrea Gabrieli, Giovanni Croce, Luca Marenzio are
the typical masters of the period, and their music is full of delight.
Never too difficult to perform, never too demanding on the listener, it
was the music so much admired by Thomas Morley and his English
contemporaries when they discovered it ten years later.

There was, perhaps, just one portent of things to come. In the early
part of the decade there is evidence that a revival of religious feeling was
on its way. Some of the most ardent church music of Palestrina (whose
Assumpta est Maria Mass dates from this period) and Lassus (whose
religious melancholia was now affecting him) was produced at this time.
For the devout, the madrigal with religious words was coming into
fashion, and even so secular a composer as Marenzio was following the
vogue. For most of the madrigalists at least, it was a polite fashion.
Christ was the good shepherd and not very different from Thyrsis; nor
was Mary a different species from Phyllis weeping for the loss of her
beloved. Nevertheless the extravagance of the Counter-Reformation is

---

1 *Le Istitutioni Harmoniche* (Venice, 1559), p. 339.

never far away and there are hints that the period of moral purpose is not yet quite over.

Monteverdi, typically enough (as it will appear), chose to begin his madrigalian career with some of these *madrigali spirituali*. He had already produced some Latin motets for three voices when, in July 1583, his new volume was in the hands of a printer in Brescia. The young man was very serious. In his preface he already looked to Plato to justify his art:

> To the Most Illustrious Gentleman and My Most Gracious Patron, Signor Alessandro Fraganesco.
>
> In view of the great love I bear for Your Excellency, I must give these pieces to no one but you, both because of the rare and infinite qualities that reside in you, and especially because in music (praised so ardently and at such length by Plato) I have not been able to compose anything better than these my first efforts for four voices, even though these first fruits I have brought forth are insipid and badly made . . .

The music survives only in a fragmentary form, but this youthful seriousness is evident from the fragments. So is its charm. There are no hints of wild chromatic passion, none of exciting devil-may-care rhythms. Nor does the verse seem to demand such extremes. Most of it is typical of the colourless religious verse of the time, no doubt sincere but lacking the power either of imagery or of thought which such subjects should inspire.

Still, Monteverdi was hardly old enough to deal with any really passionate verse at the time, and within a year he had chosen more suitable poetry to match his experience in a book of canzonets, this time printed by one of the greatest publishers of the time, the firm of Vincenti and Amadino in Venice (1584). The title page has the words 'Deo gratias' at its head, the dedication prays that 'God will grant every contentment and happiness' to Monteverdi's patron. There were no other hints of devotion. The canzonet, to quote Morley again, was a

> little short song (wherein little art can be showed, being made in strains, the beginning of which is some point lightly touched and every strain repeated except the middle) which is, in composition of the music, a counterfeit of the Madrigal.[1]

1 Op. cit., p. 295.

Its verse was light, the music uncomplicated, as indeed it had to be in a strophic form. In the hands of a master of light music (Andrea Gabrieli being perhaps the greatest of all) it might acquire a hint of irony, become something of a caricature, both in the choice of verse and in the mock-learning of its music. In the 1580s it was usually a little more sentimental, and Marenzio often made it a miniature descriptive piece, or a healthily unpassionate love song. It was just the thing to help a beginner (especially a boy) to acquire a fluent technique.

Or was it? Monteverdi's volume raises one or two doubts. A number of his pieces are admittedly quite alluring. In 'Son questi i crespi crini?' the poetaster admires the curls, the eyes, the lips, the smile of the beloved. The verse is unpretentious, the music matches it with a charmingly tuneful melody, touched only by a hint of counterpoint. Everything is regular, and orderly, with no dissonance and melodic awkwardness to disturb its innocence. 'Il mio martir tengo' is equally in tune with the verse, for neither Monteverdi nor his poet takes the lover's interruption too tragically. The music takes to the minor key and is not above a touch of imitation here and there, but the proportions are kept suitable for the miniature scale imposed by the genre. This is exactly where the doubts arise in some other numbers. 'La fiera vista', for instance, is surely too learned. The opening phrase is imitated quickly between the parts, and the first soprano has to hurry through her words in an unexpressive way to catch up with the others. The final section eclipses the tune by displaying it both the right way up and upside down almost simultaneously. Obviously Monteverdi requires space to work in and this is something which applies to much of his later work too. He is less good at the miniature or the purely lighthearted. In fact Monteverdi's true vocation is apparent in two of the more delightful of these canzonets. 'Tu ridi sempre mai' is significantly the only one which is not strophic. Its single verse allows the composer to set it without thought for succeeding strophes. Word-painting is therefore in order. Monteverdi takes the hint. The word 'ridi' (smile) provides a melisma which makes the singer appropriately part his lips; the phrase 'per darmi pena e guai' (to give me pain and sorrow) cries out for dissonance:

Ex. 1

Word-painting is clearly already one of his main preoccupations. It is only the fact that strophic songs rarely provide the opportunity for it which restrains him elsewhere; and in 'Godi pur del bel sen felice' he shows tremendous dexterity when he realises that the second line of each verse has the word 'saltando' (leaping) or 'scherzando' (joking), a chance for a gorgeously syncopated phrase to banter its way through the gaiety of the dance-song. It is such touches that show him to be searching for a more expansive form – the madrigal itself.

He may have been composing madrigals by this time, for although his *First Book of Madrigals for Five Voices* only came out three years later, a detailed examination of its contents reveals some disparity in competence and technique, suggesting that it was a collection of pieces composed over several years. One or two of these madrigals indeed hint that writing for five voices caused the student some problems. These perhaps came out of the nature of Monteverdi's education. His teacher, as all his title pages had so far proclaimed, was the *maestro di cappella* of Cremona Cathedral, Marc'Antonio Ingegneri. Ingegneri was primarily a composer of church music, and one of the old school to whom counterpoint was of some importance. His own madrigals are, on the whole, composed in the older spirit, with long breathing melodies and soundly based harmony. They are what might be called 'well written'; but they lack any of the lightness of the modern 'Marenzian' style, with its interest in colour and its delight in strongly rhythmic motives and phrases. Although Ingegneri sometimes sets pastoral verse of an up-to-date kind, his touch is heavy. There is none of the playfulness which is so essential an ingredient of the 1580s.

Monteverdi seems to have been torn between the style of his teacher and that which he must have known from more 'contemporary' music. 'Usciam, ninfe, homai fuor di questi boschi' shows the dichotomy at its clearest. The choice of poem is typical of the modern composer. It has strong imagery to inspire him to word-painting, is concentrated and short to allow him a tight construction. Monteverdi obviously knows what is to be done with the images. The word 'fiori' (flowers) has an appropriate melisma, a touch of *fioritura*; 'giro' (turn) clusters itself round a single note; at the sound of dance music, Monteverdi breaks into triple time. All this is modern in style as are the bright vocal colour of the ensemble, and the tendency to pair off the voices in little duets (something much favoured by Andrea Gabrieli). Yet there is a slightly disorganised feeling about the whole. For one thing, the proportions are not quite right. There is far too much material for such a short piece; a more experienced composer would have extended the use of each theme much more. For another, where the images do not command the composer's attention, there is very little interest. The opening section is particularly badly arranged, with Monteverdi obviously a little embarrassed by the plenitude of five voices. Four, one feels, would have been quite sufficient, as first one and then another dashes in and out of the texture, appropriately perhaps for a poem in which the nymphs are dashing out of the woods – but most unsatisfying for the musician who wants some solid development of the thematic material.

Such ill digested modernism must surely be the work of the young student, whose master was not really equipped to show him the way he wanted to go, and several numbers – 'Poi che del mio dolore', 'Filli cara e amata' and 'Se per havervi oimè' particularly – show similar inexperience in varying degrees. But since Monteverdi's dedication of the volume was written on New Year's Day 1587, when he was still nineteen, perhaps this is not surprising, and other madrigals in the book are very much better considered. 'Baci soavi e cari' is a thoroughly up-to-date piece with the modernism now fully integrated. The verse is perhaps more suitable than was that of 'Usciam, ninfe, homai fuor di questi boschi' which had a plethora of images to deal with. Here the main ideas are the beloved's kisses (mentioned three times) and the lover's 'death' – the thinly veiled convention for consummation of love – which image is also repeated. Having just two main concepts for which to find an appropriate musical expression, the difficulties of shape and proportion are quite manageable, and Monteverdi handles them extremely well. The kisses are expressed by a cadence figure which means that the sections are clearly defined, 'death' by a series of dissonances ('but never so severe as to offend') all coming out of a conventional counterpoint of which Ingegneri might have approved.

Ex. 2

In case such a passage should suggest a tragedy out of proportion to the lighthearted pastoral love of the poem, Monteverdi is careful not to make the next mention of the death wish too extended, especially since the madrigal is to be conventional in structure, with a final section repeated in the manner of a large scale canzonet. And in this repetition Monteverdi shows his craftsmanship. Many composers would have repeated the material exactly, perhaps with some minor changing around of the voices (the two soprano lines are often reversed). Not Monteverdi. If the repetition begins exactly, the cadence at the end of the first line of verse is hurried on so as to increase the tension – and hurried on to a variant of the second line in which a simple three-part texture is amplified with a tutti. Even the cadence at the end of the section is altered, so that the twinge of dissonant desire which is just right for the middle of the madrigal is softened down so as to relax at the very end of the piece. 'Baci soavi e cari' is not a great masterpiece; it is too slight for that (and should be treated more as a canzonetta than a serious madrigal in performance). It is, nevertheless, the work of a master.

Monteverdi's ambitions are clear elsewhere in the volume, in a cycle of three linked madrigals, 'Ardo, si, ma non t'amo', 'Ardi o gela a tua voglia' and 'Arsi e alsi a mia voglia'. Madrigal cycles were the secular composer's answer to the problem of scale. The church musician could set the five movements of the Ordinary of the Mass if he wanted to produce a large, ambitious work. The Magnificat and some of the long psalms offered an equal challenge to the composer anxious to get away from the miniature. The madrigalist had fewer opportunities, although in the early days of the genre it was not uncommon to set an extended poem of Petrarch in several musical sections; and later, composers sometimes chose verse with a common theme to give shape and unity to a complete madrigal book. Monteverdi's first try at such a cycle was a popular one in the 1580s. The first two poems were set many times. They consist of the lover's attempt to shrug off his beloved's indifference. 'I burn, but do not love you. My ardour is that of disdain, not of love', he sings. His lady knows better. 'Burn or freeze, just as you will; your disdain is of no account, for your heart is affected nevertheless'. Ingegneri had set these poems, although he was scarcely the sort of man to do it really effectively. Monteverdi must have known his setting, and actually borrows a theme or two from his master; but he is slightly more expansive. He adds yet a third poem: 'love or hate, it doesn't really matter; both are in vain'. Clearly the die is cast, and the final poem is a good idea to sum up the other two. It does, however, add something to the musician's burden. He could write contrasting madrigals if setting just the first poem and its *risposta* (reply). Add a *contrarisposta* (counter-reply) and some unifying factor must be found. By now Monteverdi is quite capable of this. His opening madrigal is rather like Ingegneri, contrapuntal and not too expressive, not very modern but attractive enough, especially when it arrives at the final words 'I burn with anger, not with love', which give rise to a delightful *concertante* interplay between various groups of voices. The beginning of the second madrigal is also Ingegneri-like (there is a touching piece of academicism in the opening bars with a bit of close imitation and an inversion crowded together as in Monteverdi's canzonets). Then we realise why Monteverdi has provided his *concertante* section in the first piece at such length: it is to be the link between the two. Not that the repetition is to be exact. As in 'Baci soavi e cari', Monteverdi re-works his material so as never to surrender the element of surprise, but the theme holds the two pieces together in such a way that it is quite impossible to perform either by itself. But just in case there should be any doubt that the *contrarisposta* is to follow, Monteverdi turns the full cadence of the first section into an inconclusive ending on the dominant chord in the second. Here the real problem emerges. To repeat the *concertante* section once again would surely result in monotony, yet some other link must be found. Again a lively imagination is at work. The lover was the speaker in the first piece, his beloved in the second. As he returns with his counter-reply, what is more natural than for the opening of the first madrigal to open the third? So it does: not exactly, of course – it is treated quite differently, but it is the same theme, and it makes the necessary point.

Ex. 3

This time the lover's anger is softened and the *concertante* section, with its contrasting groupings, gives way to a more contrapuntal attitude. Monteverdi's next surprise comes at the end. Instead of the expected full cadence to round off the cycle, he repeats that which concluded the second madrigal. The word 'insano' (unhealthy – a reference to the lover's wounded heart) is the link here, and if at first the inconclusiveness looks like a mistake, a little reflection reveals Monteverdi's intention. The madrigal cycle may be at an end, yet the banter of courtship is going to continue for some time. Did these lovers ever come together? Or is it that the continual renewal of courtship is very much part of love? Monteverdi leaves us with a delicious enigma.

This cycle is the first sign that Monteverdi was to be concerned with finding satisfactory musical forms for his grand conceptions. Probably he would have denied this preoccupation, saying, as he did so often in later life, that his main concern was with the expression of the words: *prima le parole, poi la musica*. We may have fewer scruples about considering him a consummate musician. Certainly it is a considerable advance in musicianship which makes his *Second Book of Madrigals for Five Voices* such an interesting volume. It took him the three years to 1590 to complete this collection (the dedication is again dated New Year's Day) and on the title page of its first edition Monteverdi still acknowledges that he is a 'disciple of Signor Ingegneri'. The contents, however, suggest that he is fast outgrowing his master. One or two madrigals, notably 'Cantai un tempo, e se fu dolc'il canto', 'Bevea Fillide mia' and perhaps 'Dolcissimi legami di parole amorose' derive their style from that of Ingegneri. Elsewhere everything is much more up-to-date. The choice of verse, the kind of treatment it receives, the texture, the thematic material, all are quite different from those of the *First Book*. Clearly something has happened to change Monteverdi's attitude.

The most likely explanation is that he had been travelling outside his native Cremona. Although throughout his life Monteverdi tended to retire to his father's house when in trouble, a fact which suggests that his father was well enough off to keep him, he was certainly looking for employment. There was none very profitable, either financially or emotionally, in provincial Cremona. We know that Monteverdi had links in Milan, and that he played his viol (or violin, it is not clear which) in the house of his patron there. We know, too, that there was casual employment to be had at the courts of the Gonzagas at Mantua not far away. It seems more than probable that he visited Mantua and perhaps even Ferrara, only a little farther off, on professional engagements.

This would certainly explain why a number of new elements have come into his style. The most obvious of these is the new prominence now given to the upper voices. At Ferrara, there was a famous ensemble of three ladies who sang trios specially written by the court musicians to show off their dexterous voices. Nearby Mantua also had some prima donnas of considerable skill, and its principal composer, the Nether-lander Giaches de Wert, had fallen in love – not just metaphorically – with one of the Ferrara ladies. He wrote a great deal of music for this ensemble, and we shall find Monteverdi quite consciously imitating him. Another feature which now dominates his music is the sheer delight in timbre for its own sake. This indicates that, like the composers of these fine musical courts, he is writing for the listener as well as the performer. In domestic chamber music (which is probably what his first madrigals were intended to be) counterpoint provides an equality of parts which is very pleasing for the performer. But it cannot be denied that it can be confusing for the ear. Attention to the actual quality of sound is what the listener needs, and now Monteverdi is obviously very interested in it. Finally, the actual verse which he sets comes from the court circles. Tasso and Guarini both lived for a time in Mantua and Ferrara. Although their work does appear occasionally in Ingegneri's music, it became really fashionable, predictably enough, with the composers with whom they lived at the Gonzaga and d'Este courts. There are signs that Monteverdi now knows much more of their verse, and is attracted by it.

The new style can be seen at once in the first number of the madrigal book, 'Non si levav' ancor l'alba novella'. The verse is a typical piece of Tasso: full of concrete imagery which is linked strongly to the emotional state of the lover. 'The dawn was not yet rising', sings the poet, presenting the composer with a puzzle. How does one set the fact that it was *not* rising? Monteverdi has a brilliant solution. He presents a twin motive (a characteristic of the modern school, such as Andrea Gabrieli and Marenzio). The soprano descends, the tenor rises:

Ex. 4

The birds are still sleeping (a gently undulating phrase), the two lovers (believe it or not, a duet!) have enjoyed a sweet night under the stars – an opportunity for Monteverdi to break into 'black notation' with all the notes filled in[1] – a quite usual method of indicating triple time. And so

1   In this notation a semibreve is written as ●

it goes on. Each image suggests some new musical idea, and Monteverdi is at his most inventive. But it is not the invention which is most remarkable; it is his new mastery of form. Each phrase is now given adequate opportunity to develop. He has a flair for combining the voices to give new sounds while continuing with his thematic material, and his repetition of the themes of the opening section at the end of the madrigal, although perhaps borrowed from the French *chanson* which often used this device, shows his economical frame of mind. As in the madrigal cycle of the *First Book*, Monteverdi does not rest content until he has bound together his linked madrigals (for one sets the octave, the other the sestet of the sonnet), and sure enough when the dawn does finally arrive there is a strong hint of the first motives.

There are several numbers in the book in this vein, and all are extremely attractive. The most famous is undoubtedly 'Ecco mormorar l'onde', another setting of Tasso and one which uses every bit of poetic imagery to inspire music equally pictorial. Not a point is missed: the gentle movement of the waves, the melismatic song of the birds, the smiling Orient, the high mountains and every other detail find appropriate musical motives. Indeed it is almost too extrovert for Monteverdi, and it is only when we compare it with a sister piece by Giaches de Wert, 'Vezzosi augelli' (to another of Tasso's poems), that we begin to see the young man developing his own distinctive voice. Both madrigals are extremely alike in attitude, in invention, in the bright tonality, the magic of the vocal *concertante* interplay, so alike that we may assume Monteverdi knew the other piece. Yet Wert stops at pictorialism. His madrigal is purely external and descriptive. Monteverdi follows him fairly closely until the final line of the poem:

> . . . with the dawn comes its messenger,
> the breeze which cools each feverish heart.

The 'feverish heart' is too strong a suggestion for Monteverdi to miss. The lightheartedness of the madrigal is dismissed. Slow, dissonant motion is brought in to conclude the piece; and at once a personal, introverted mood appears. It is not exaggerated. Monteverdi takes less than a dozen bars to make his point – and he could have repeated his concluding section if he had wanted to, for this was not an unusual procedure. Nevertheless, Monteverdi's interests are clear. Similarly, the gaiety of 'S' andasse amor a caccia', in which the image of the hunt provokes lively rhythms and, naturally, some vivid canonic writing, is just a little interrupted by a few dissonances near the end. 'Non giacinti o narcisi' equally loses its very attractive innocence as the lover warms to his beloved's charms.

These are probably the best things in this madrigal book, for they seem to match the unsentimental attitude of the young man, still only twenty-two and not yet much buffeted by fate. Even so, his technical grasp is such that setting more serious verse is now by no means beyond his grasp. 'Crudel, perchè mi fuggi?' was a poem recently (1587) set by the Mantuan composer Benedetto Pallavicino. Pallavicino's setting was a good enough madrigal to be chosen by Nicholas Yonge, singing man of St Paul's, for his second volume of *Musica Transalpina* (1597), in which the verse appears in the following excellently close translation:

> Cruell, why dost thou flye mee,
> If so my death so great content may winne thee,
> Thou hast my hart within thee,
> Dost *thou* thinck by thy flying
> Cruell, to see mee dying?
> Oh, none alyve can die hurtlesse, ungrieved,
> And griefe can no man feele, of hart deprived.

Such verse offers no easy way of putting it to music. Such concrete images as there are (and 'to fly' offers the only real opportunity for pictorialism) are irrelevant to the overall mood. Moreover, the singlemindedness of the poem is a temptation to monotonous slow movement which will overdo the sentiment. After all, the flirtations of Guarini's lovers usually end happily, and this is no tragic lament. Monteverdi does well by the poem. He begins with a slow movement, but although the minor harmonies set the mood at once, there is no exaggeration, no severe dissonance or chromaticism. He also gives himself adequate space in which to develop his ideas. Each phrase is repeated, usually with some change of texture to keep it alive; and the climax in the last line, which seems to need considerable expansion, gains its power by starting a minor third above the initial announcement on its re-statement. It is again the work of a craftsman, and a craftsman who now sees what the modern idiom has to offer. Counterpoint is less interesting than the *concertante* interplay of vocal groupings in this style. Monteverdi is beginning to master the technique of vocal 'orchestration'.

As we have seen, this interest was undoubtedly fostered by Monteverdi's new-found knowledge of the virtuoso ensembles of the nearby courts, and one or two pieces reflect his fascination with the bright colours they offered the composer. 'Intorno a due vermiglie e vaghe labra' begins with a dozen bars in which the three upper voices are used, and although the men's voices then enter, they tend to remain a supporting group rather than full participants in the thematic material. The three ladies emerge frequently from the *tutti* to form by themselves a coherent ensemble, and the effect is splendid. In 'Dolcemente dormiva la mia Clori', the predominance of the upper voices is not quite so strong but it is quite noticeable that the more ornamental material is confined to them, and there is still a feeling that the sopranos and alto are considered a unified group. Something of this attitude is evident even in 'Crudel, perchè mi fuggi?', although here the role of the upper group is to contrast with the lower trio (the alto acting as a go-between) and the texture is anything but crude.

In this, Monteverdi's *Second Book* has obviously been written after the composer had become acquainted with the music of Wert, and perhaps Luzzasco Luzzaschi, who was the principal composer for the Three Ladies of Ferrara. But there is a significant difference between the madrigals of Luzzaschi and Wert on the one hand, and Monteverdi on the other. The older composers write for singers who were very accomplished. They write roulades and decorative lines of various kinds which need a considerable vocal dexterity. Monteverdi never does. At their most difficult his soprano lines are never beyond the singer of moderate attainments. They are most gratefully written and must give delight to any amateur who attempts them. Indeed, what difficulties do exist in this book (and they are few) come in the parts of the tenor and bass, whose range is occasionally taxed, and who are given an occasional awkward leap, as in 'E dicea l'una sospirando' where the tenor is expected at times to change from his upper to his lower register with undue haste. These signs indicate Monteverdi's predicament. Probably at Cremona the best singers available were those of the cathedral, the singing men whose main musical experience was of old-fashioned church music. As long as he stayed there, the opportunities for becoming a 'modern' were strictly limited. The madrigals of this period in his life are most attractive for the amateur (those of the *Second Book* should especially be better known to the English madrigal groups). The Italian composer, at least, is honest enough to know that greatness lies elsewhere.

Mannerism at Mantua

Monteverdi finally settled at Mantua at some time between the publication of his *Second Book of Madrigals* and the appearance of the *Third* in 1592. No doubt it seemed a great step forward at the time. No doubt it was also not very long before he regretted his apparent promotion. For if the court of the Gonzagas was a focal point for many musicians at this time, it was an unpleasant place to work. The climate was (and remains) bad, too hot in the summer, with a high humidity caused by the marshy lakes which surrounded the city, and too cold in winter, when the Po valley can be exceedingly foggy. Monteverdi complained about it constantly. The claustrophobic atmosphere can still be felt, with the small market-town completely dominated by the huge palace of the Dukes. There was no way of avoiding the moods of the reigning prince, and Vincenzo I was not the most stable of employers. There was more than a touch of madness in the Mantuan atmosphere, with the disproportion between the apparent wealth of the ruling house, its style of living far exceeding in opulence that of the Doges of Venice or the Sforzas of Milan, and the power it really had in the world outside – which was very little indeed.

Still, the Gonzagas had been great patrons of the arts for generations. The frescoes in their *Sala degli Sposi* were by Mantegna; their country home had been designed and decorated by Giulio Romano; Rubens was their court painter during Monteverdi's time in their service. They had good taste in music too. They had tried to tempt Palestrina and Marenzio to direct their music, but both were disinclined to leave their comfortable surroundings in Rome. Wert, their *maestro di cappella*, was a most distinguished composer. Gastoldi, who was in charge of music in their private chapel of S. Barbara, was the most famous composer of light music of the time. Of their virtuoso singers, Adriana Basile was one of the greatest prima donnas of the day. Monteverdi was in good company. In the choice of these artists of various kinds, the private world of the Gonzagas is well mirrored. The feeling of instability is there. It is no coincidence that mannerist painting flourished in Mantua (and to a lesser degree in its sister courts at Parma, Ferrara and Florence where similar conditions existed). It is typical that exaggerated emotionalism was encouraged: the very air seemed overwrought. The Gonzaga household was abnormal and bizarre, and had created an artificial world of sensationalism. The Hall of Mirrors in the Palazzo Ducale is a symptom of the disease, in its attempt to make itself appear much larger than life, and distorting reality in the process. Their poets matched this atmosphere in many ways, and as we read the erotic poems of Guarini or his *Il Pastor Fido*, with its constantly weeping shepherds and shepherdesses, the feeling of alienation increases.

So far as the musicians went, they could to some extent escape this. Their church music remained well balanced and Gastoldi's lightheartedness is sincerely felt, even in that hint of irony which so often infects the canzonettas and villanellas of the sixteenth century. But Wert at least succumbed to mannerism, especially in his later madrigal books. This was not surprising. He had arrived in Italy at the time when Cipriano de Rore was the fashionable composer, and had been deeply affected by the first revolution in madrigalian style. From his earliest days at Mantua, he was interested in the expression of extreme emotions. His very first madrigals show him the master of strong contrasts and bold musical images. By the time Monteverdi arrived in Mantua, he was almost a musical eccentric. Although quite capable of writing in a conventional manner, many of his madrigals are full of strange quirks. Educated to believe that words should always be audible he wrote some pieces which take to the principle of recitative, and push the idea to its logical conclusion so as to neglect practically all ordinary musical devices. In others he felt that violent words require violent expression. His method in these was to use melody so awkward that it is a plague to the singer. Diminished intervals, wildly wide leaps, chromaticisms were all grist to his mill. Some madrigals demand singers with such a large *tessitura* that virtuosity is a *sine qua non* for their performance. In all of them there is a nervous discontinuity which seems to match the Mantuan atmosphere. Wert was not the only revolutionary among the madrigalists. The spirit of the latter years of the 1580s and of the last decade of the century encouraged gloom and extremism, and even so stable a composer as Marenzio was influenced by it. The younger ones, especially those at Mantua, could hardly avoid this musical mannerism. Certainly Monteverdi caught up rapidly with the vogue for modernism. Within months of arriving at the court, he had dedicated a new book of madrigals to his new lord and master. And what a change of style there has been! The most obvious sign is contained in his choice of poetry. No longer will he set the verse of nonentities. Tasso and Guarini dominate the book – and it is now not the innocent nature-pieces which interest him, but their highly emotional erotica. 'Crudel, perchè mi fuggi?' had been the 'advanced' poem of the *Second Book*; in the *Third*, it would be the norm. It is no coincidence that these are the very poems which had tempted Wert to extremism. Monteverdi from the start clearly admired the 'excellent Signor Giaches' (to quote one of his letters) and wished to emulate him.

It is equally obvious that his newly-found virtuoso singers have inspired Monteverdi. The three-madrigal cycle 'Vattene pur, crudel, con quella pace' is not to be tackled by the unskilful, for it makes demands on the musicianship of each singer. Whatever the pitch or degree of transposition in use at Mantua 'O dolce anima mia' asks for at least one voice with a fully developed range. The expressive use of the monotone at the opening of 'Se per estremo ardore morir potesse un core' requires a singer more than usually sensitive to true intonation. Even the pieces which are nearest Monteverdi's youthful style develop that tendency to use *fioritura* in the upper voices which we have already seen in 'Dolcemente dormiva la mia Clori' and 'Intorno a due vermiglie e vaghe labra'. The very first number in the book, 'La giovinetta pianta si fa più bell' al sole', has a section for the upper three voices that must derive from the style of the Ferrarese ladies, 'Lumi miei, cari lumi' is full of their dexterity and must surely have been meant for some such ensemble. There is no sign at all of men's voices for more than a dozen bars at its opening:

Ex. 5

'O come è gran martire' is only to be recommended to madrigal groups which can provide three evenly matched women's voices who can sing perfectly in tune, for their parts are very exposed and, since each sings all the significant material at the same pitch, any divergence from the true shows up with startling clarity.

Virtuosity is rarely profound: nor are such madrigals. But delightful as these frothy pieces are, Monteverdi undoubtedly was making his most strenuous efforts in becoming a serious composer. This shows in places where it is quite unexpected. 'Sovra tenere herbette e bianchi fiori' is a charming piece of pastoral nonsense, in which the love-making of Phyllis and her shepherd is delicately portrayed as a joyful, undemanding activity. Monteverdi's short canzonet-like phrases dance with strong, memorable rhythms; the newly-found sonority of the women's voices creates a splendidly sunny atmosphere. The temptation to over-paint Thyrsis' plea for haste is resisted, as the time is not yet ripe. Then at the end the poet suggests the urgency of the situation as Phyllis cries 'Oh kiss me, my Thyrsis, kiss me for I feel myself dying too' (the sixteenth century had no doubts whatever of the reality of feminine desire). The poet stresses this scarcely at all. Monteverdi on the other hand makes it really passionate. He first of all builds up the tension with a pedal over which the kisses come faster and faster. Then he slows down such activity, and Phyllis languishes in the classic way, in sevenths and semibreves. Surely she must now be granted peace; but no, Monteverdi repeats the whole section, kisses and all. Moreover this time the matter is serious. Phyllis again languishes in semibreves, but to the sevenths are added seconds and double suspensions. The relief of the final cadence suddenly becomes very welcome.

Such passages occur quite frequently in this volume. The warblings of the nightingale in 'O rossignol ch'in queste verdi fronde' are prettily expressed in its opening trio section, the two sopranos especially displaying their grace. They are there only to contrast with the lover's anguish, and with the use of the first person in the verse enter the dissonances of the musician, made more intense by ambiguities of tonality, as B natural and B flat vie within the space of a couple of bars. This piece admittedly ends happily, which is more than can be said of 'O primavera, gioventù de l'anno', in which springtime ardour is seen to bring its troubles, and the slowly moving conclusion is full of tough, if transitory, discords. Nor is 'Ch'io non t'ami, cor mio', in spite of both the canzonetta syncopations which jauntily open it and its music for the Three Ladies, entirely free from a more serious vein; and its concluding bars have some effectively sustained suspensions.

These madrigals are some of the most enjoyable Monteverdi wrote. The tinge of fashionable melancholy adds spice to the predominant gaiety without becoming artificial or neurotic. Their straightforward tonality, crisp rhythmic motives, tuneful brief phrases make them such a constant delight to the singer that it can hardly fail to transmit itself to the listener. Not all the madrigals of this *Third Book* are so fortunately written. 'Stracciami pur il core', for example, begins in the same sort of style, the conventional rhythm derived from the French *chanson* firmly setting the cheerful mood. It is soon interrupted by severe discords – a ninth and seventh. The *chanson* motive is tried again, this time interrupted by more dissonance, and dissonance which lasts a score of bars. Lighter relief is provided by some rather aimless counterpoint, but the discords resume: 'I cannot die of love . . .'. This is a fine climax, ten bars of almost continuous dissonance, the culmination of which is a particularly vicious chord with four adjacent notes of the scale crushed against one another.

Ex. 6

Monteverdi cannot end this way. He takes the suggestion of the poet: out of such death comes love's felicity. More canzonet phrases are worked out contrapuntally, the final cadence is made suitably more harsh than usual, but this discord is quickly despatched and does not seem to belong to the same world as those so drawn out earlier. And this is precisely what is disturbing about this madrigal. The climactic phrase is so remarkable that the theorist Padre Martini was to quote it in the eighteenth century to demonstrate how revolutionary Monteverdi was; and the other extravagances are only slightly less convincing. What goes on in between is much less memorable, even to the point of being undistinguished. Monteverdi fails to make the proportions between the two moods at all balanced.

If 'Stracciami pur il core' is a problematic madrigal, the two parts of 'Rimanti in pace a la dolente e bella Fillida' can only be described as eccentric. Again the initial idea is conventional enough: the word 'pace' (peace) suggests a slow moving common chord, and as Thyrsis speeds to his grieving ('dolente') Phyllis, it is natural to convey both her sorrow (by minor harmonies) and his sighs (by putting a rest in the middle of the word 'sospirando', so that the singer has to catch his breath). But already the dangers are becoming obvious. Monteverdi has painted in music three poetic images within the shortest possible space. If he continues in this way, it will be the detail rather than the broader emotional expression which will command the listener's attention. So it does. Every time the word 'aspra' (harsh) comes in setting the next line of the verse, there must be a dissonance – and 'aspra' is repeated a dozen times. The succeeding phrase makes the suggestion of 'amaro' (bitter): this time it is a chromatic fragment of melody which is imitated throughout the five voices. There is even less peace for the lovers in the second part, 'Ond' ei di morte la sua faccia impressa'. 'Death' receives its deserts in a suddenly chromatic modulation (this is very effective) and when a diatonic phrase for the upper voices emerges from this, there is for a moment a breath of fresh air. Gloom immediately returns. The martyrdom of the lover revives not only the chromaticism but also the dissonance. To count the number of 'martyrdoms' expressed in this way would be a tedious occupation, but the general effect is certainly confused by this plethora of expressionism. The clarity of tonality is admittedly established in the final phrase, and it is interesting that one characteristic of the mature Monteverdian style is used freely in it. The downward sixth leap is to become one of his most attractive means of achieving pathos (see Ex. 7 overleaf). Here, oddly enough, it seems very mild compared with what has gone before.

The Mantuan atmosphere has surely gone to Monteverdi's head, and in the largest enterprise of the volume, the madrigal cycle 'Vattene pur,

Ex. 7

crudel, con quella pace', the reasons for his change of style become obvious. For this is a work very close in manner to the later music of Giaches de Wert. The signs are unmistakable. Like Wert, Monteverdi is here intrigued by the possibilities of choral recitative. Many of his 'motives' (if such they can be called) consist of monotones, the words given rhythm in a casual way, the syllables crowded indeterminately on the single note. When leaps from this monotone are taken for expressive purposes, they tend to be wide, awkward intervals, or at least awkwardly arranged successions of intervals. The whole attitude to the melody is deliberately ungrateful to the singer, the extremes of the voice frequently in use, the unexpected turn of phrase sometimes very difficult to pitch or to control in tune. Like some of Wert's madrigals, it seems almost anti-musical; and this it was probably meant to be. It is the first major attempt Monteverdi has made to obey the dicta of the Greeks: that music is to be the servant of the words and not their master. The words must be audible – hence the recitative; they must be expressed – hence the bizarre intervals. It was as simple as that. Or at least it should have been as simple as that, for Monteverdi contemplated this principle for the rest of his life, and had no intellectual doubts about its essential truth. In practice it was not so easy to forget all that he had learned from his master, Marc'Antonio Ingegneri. Even in 'Vattene pur, crudel, con quella pace' real music will keep appearing. The word 'l'onde' (wave) may command a 'wavy', melismatic phrase: it scarcely can command that it be worked out thoroughly between the voices in the older polyphonic manner. The chromatic phrase which expresses grief in the second section 'Là tra 'l sang' e le morti' may be suggested by the words, but the musician is well in control in its development, which is much more securely based tonally than anything in 'Rimanti in pace a la dolente e bella Fillida'. The inconclusive endings of the first two sections, so as to link the three madrigals firmly together, reminds us of the technique of 'Ardo, si, ma non t'amo' in the *First Book*. Deprived of vital melody it may be, but Monteverdi knows that variety can be obtained by a constant change of texture. By the final section, 'Poi ch'ella in sè tornò', he is working in a series of trios to contrast with the *tutti* in a most imaginatively musical way. Music the 'servant of the words' indeed!

Nevertheless this madrigal cycle is a strange work, the disproportion among its elements of expression and recitative too evident to both performers and listeners. Perhaps it is not surprising that such a radical change of direction should not yield satisfactory results straight away, and we must remember that Monteverdi can have been acquainted with such modernism for only two years at the most – and it may in fact have been no more than a matter of months. Experimental techniques take time to acquire. We must also suspect that Monteverdi was not yet emotionally ready for musical mannerism. Wert, with his disappointment in love (not to mention his thirty years with the Gonzagas), might have been able to set the words of another of Monteverdi's mannerist cycles 'Vivrò fra i miei tormenti e le mie cure' (I shall live with my torments) with some depth of feeling. It is hard to imagine that his young colleague, at the age of twenty-five a real, if modest, success, had quite the same incentive. It was only now that the roughness of life at Mantua began to reveal the edges.

What little we know of Monteverdi's next ten years indicates they were less happy. He had two opportunities for foreign travel. He went with the Mantuan troops to the battlefields of Hungary to help soothe his master on the campaign against the Turks. It was not a glorious campaign (the Gonzaga contingent saw little action), and, as he tells us in a later letter, while Monteverdi was honoured by the compliment, he was also paid inadequately. Much the same happened when the Duke went to the Netherlands a few years later on more pleasurable pursuits. Monteverdi, now married, felt the financial pinch even harder. By this time a professional disappointment had helped to embitter him. In 1596 Wert died. Monteverdi almost certainly expected the job, but his colleague Benedetto Pallavicino was given it instead. Pallavicino was, of course, an older man of greater experience, and in any case lasted only another five years. This did not prevent Monteverdi feeling slighted.

Nor was the musician so confident now. In the nine years between 1583 and 1592 Monteverdi had produced five volumes of various kinds of music amounting to over a hundred pieces. It took him the next thirteen years to have fifty pieces ready for the press. There are signs in his letters that he had to write occasional music for dramatic entertainments and church festivals. This may have taken up some of his time, yet it hardly explains why, although he had hoped to have his *Fourth Book of Madrigals* ready in the lifetime of Alfonso d'Este (he says in his dedication that he wanted to present it to this great patron of music), it in fact only appeared some six years after Alfonso's death. It cannot be imagined that his publisher was reluctant. The *Third Book* achieved a second edition, in 1594, and by three years later Monteverdi's music was beginning to appear in various popular anthologies. He even composed some canzonets for one collector, Antonio Morsolino, which are quite charming, though typically enough rather more serious than they need have been. It looks as though some spiritual crisis took place, some failure of fluency. The next news of Monteverdi's madrigals in fact arrives from another quarter. In the year 1600 a monk living in Bologna, Father Giovanni Maria Artusi, came out with an attack on 'modern music'; and the spearhead of this attack was directed against Monteverdi. In particular, one madrigal, a setting of a lament from Guarini's *Il Pastor Fido*, called down Artusi's wrath. 'Cruda Amarilli' was full of the most shocking dissonance, according to him. He quoted nine extracts (taken freely from their contexts) and pulled them to bits. His criteria are, by the standards of 1600, very old-fashioned. There is no mercy in the attack and no sign that Artusi really knew any music written since about 1565. The list of authorities from whom he claims support is impressive, ranging from Aristotle to Cipriano de Rore, but he shows no idea that he had grasped their variety, nor their real aims. To compare him, say, with that other notorious critic of a great composer, Hanslick, is to realise what a puny capacity for thought Artusi really had. He was not in any way a worthy opponent of Monteverdi. Nevertheless Monteverdi clearly felt offended by the attack. He planned to write a book rebutting it, and since writing a theoretical treatise was, as he admitted nearly thirty years later, very hard work for him, we may assume that he took Artusi seriously. It is typical, perhaps, of Monteverdi that with most of the famous names of his epoch very much on his side – the Florentine theorists, the Ferrara composers, his Mantua colleagues, not to mention such a figure as Gesualdo – he had to justify himself to the world against an insignificant opponent. Again there is more than a suggestion of lack of self-confidence.

By 1603 the doubts must have receded, and never again was there such a long gap between published works. Admittedly Monteverdi's later letters tell us that he was a slow composer. The jingle 'Presto e bene, insieme non conviene' (haste and good work don't go together) occurs more than once as his excuse for delays in fulfilling commissions. The youthful period of unthinking composition was over. But what a mastery has taken its place! Both the *Fourth* and *Fifth Books* are full of some of the greatest madrigals ever written. Even those numbers nearest in style to his early music show an increase in technical grasp which makes them miniature masterpieces. 'Non più guerra, pietate', for example, is not unlike the madrigals of *Books Two* and *Three*. Its opening image of war suggests some fanfare music and some military rhythms in the pictorial vein of 'Ecco mormorar l'onde', and the idea of the love-death (sixteenth-century style) naturally produces a slow-moving contrasting section and the sixth leap which we have seen in 'Ond' ei di morte la sua faccia impressa'. The improvement in proportions is now very evident. There is no hint of exaggeration, none that the dissonance or occasional chromaticism in any way lacks direction. 'Quel augellin che canta si dolcemente' is equally charming. It is a piece with the Three Ladies very much in mind but their virtuoso carollings periodically infect the men's parts also, a sure sign that Monteverdi has a very good ensemble at his disposal. The concrete images of Boccaccio's verse each obtain their true reward, never being taken too seriously (even 'ardo' – I burn – fails to interrupt the general good humour) and the English madrigal singer will welcome it as showing the same virtuosity in combining imagery and attractive melody that Weelkes and Wilbye display at their best. An equal vitality is appropriate to 'Io mi son giovinetta', which is the largest of the Cremona-type madrigals, full of melismatic expression for such words as 'fiorisce' (flourish) and 'fuggi' (fly), and demanding both a dexterity of voice and a lightness of touch which offer a pleasant challenge to any ensemble.

These works could scarcely have been the cause of the delay in producing the *Fourth Book of Madrigals*. This lies elsewhere. We need hardly know of the quarrel between Monteverdi and Artusi to recognise that Monteverdi had been thinking deeply about the innovations of Giaches de Wert, for all the directions in which Wert had been pointing are more fully explored in this volume. The most obvious Wert-ism is the emphasis on the audibility of the words. In such madrigals as 'Cor mio, non mori?', 'Anima mia, perdona' and 'Anima dolorosa' the homophonic texture is so continuous that not a word need be lost. The way the words are set in the individual melodic lines is also an aid to understanding, for if in these pieces Monteverdi does not depart from conventional rhythms, nor crowd in a number of syllables on a single note by elisions as Wert did, he still adheres to the natural verbal accentuation. Melismas are something of an event, reserved for expressive purposes, and often are for the most part no more than short ornaments of the sort with which sixteenth-century singers often decorated their parts. Nor does the harmony divert attention from the

declamation of the verse. There are extended passages without dissonances of any kind, and chromaticism is also rare. This may sound dull
music; on the contrary, there are many methods of sustaining interest.
Monteverdi may be taking great care to make the poem clear, but this
does not prevent him from repeating separate lines of verse if a larger
musical scale is required. This allows for a greater range of colour to be
used, and these madrigals are built up as a series of varied trios and
quartets, in which the *tutti* are reserved for the climaxes. And if
dissonance is uncommon, it has great intensity when it is used. 'It is I,
not you, that feels this pain and torment' sings the poet in 'Che se tu se il
cor mio': having written some twenty bars of harmonically very
innocent homophony, Monteverdi turns the knife in the wound in a
pungent duet, where there is nothing to hide the frequent discords. In
'Cor mio, non mori?', the lack of harmonic incident has extended over
twice as long before 'Io moro' (I die) provokes similar intensity.

Ex. 8

The most extreme example of this style is also the one which best shows
its potentialities. 'Sfogava con le stelle un inferno d'amore' goes beyond
its ordinary limits because the words are literally declaimed at various
points. Monteverdi writes the notation commonly used for chanting the
psalms, and merely indicates the notes of the chord to be sung, leaving
the actual rhythms to the performers, with the obvious intention that
they should approach speech in speed and accentuation. It is, of course,
the principle of recitative, which was being developed at Florence at the
very time these madrigals were being composed. What we, with our
hindsight into the nature of recitative, find strange is that instead of
being used to express the comparatively unemotional, it is part of a
highly intense setting of a highly intense poem.

Why did Monteverdi have recourse to this experimental idiom in this
context? There are two reasons. One is that he, in common with many
composers of his generation, thought that to hear the words in itself
generated the mood of the poem; and with a highly literate audience this
was undoubtedly true. The other is that at the end of each phrase of

recitative, the elaborate music which takes over seems more vital than ever; and this, with a musical audience, is equally true. The element of surprise is ever present. At the end of the first phrase of recitative, the word 'stelle' (stars) suggests only a brief decoration in the top voice, and a constant cadence. The second adds dissonance because it must express the pain of the lover. The third has no dissonance, but the cadence has now become half a dozen bars of lively counterpoint, as the poet contemplates the eyes of his beloved. His final plea for mercy has to be made so strong that it requires three chanted phrases. The common chord of the chant at first is resolved with a simple pair of chords; then the chant is reintroduced by bringing in the lower voices half way through the recitation, so that new impetus is given to it, impetus which expands its resolution to some half a dozen bars of quite dissonant harmony; finally the chant is immediately followed by a very strong discord and a huge contrapuntal coda, full of strange harmonies needing a pedal note to calm the emotions and bring relief in a highly welcome major chord. This variety is astonishing. It reminds us of Haydn's capacity to make the recapitulation of his first subjects an endless source of amazement, as we are never sure what will happen next. Monteverdi is a consummate musician even at his most theoretical and experimental.

This musicianship is also found in the other madrigals influenced by Wert. For the mannerist attitude which results in deliberately tense melody and extreme harmony is much in evidence in *Books Four* and *Five*. There is plenty of Wert's awkwardness; sixths and sevenths are commonplace in all the melodic lines, and they have a nasty habit of going somewhere quite unexpected. Easier intervals to sing become less easy when arranged so that the whole range of the voice is used within three or four quickly moving notes. ('Era l'anima mia già presso a l'ultim' hore' has a particularly graceless tenor part because of this.) Another trial for the performer is the occasional introduction of a voice on a dissonance. Very often it does not sound particularly harsh because the note is really passed between one voice and the next so that it seems part of a continuous line. It remains still a pinprick, and certainly to the singer, using not a score but a single part-book, adds to the tension. Indeed, the increased harmonic sophistication is one of the singer's chief troubles. Monteverdi is much bolder than Wert in his free use of discord. The seventh is now considered as a normal harmony. To the ear accustomed to sixteenth-century purity, the dominant seventh chord in the final cadence of 'Che se tu se il cor mio' sounds brazenly romantic.

But there are many worse chords than this. Monteverdi often uses the effect of delaying a melody note while the bass moves on, with some very pungent sounds resulting. Having created such a dissonance, he makes it worse by refusing to take the next concord normally. His dissonant part will leap about to another note of the same chord in an embarrassing way, something enough to make the theorists turn in their graves.

None of these traits was unique to Monteverdi. One of the Florentine composers, Vincenzo Galilei (father of the astronomer), had written a harmony treatise advocating such freedom. Some of Monteverdi's Mantuan colleagues, notably the despised Benedetto Pallavicino, had used similar harsh harmonies, while the chromatic madrigals of Gesualdo, which had started appearing in print in 1596, made almost anything possible. Yet Monteverdi's combination of such things, especially when they are inserted in a music which still adheres to the basic textures and attitudes of the later sixteenth century, is quite remarkable, and it is this growth in technical device that makes possible the really astonishing feature of the madrigals of *Books Four* and *Five*, their emotional breadth. The range of treatment given to what is virtually a single subject, pastoral love, is the result of true virtuosity on the part of the composer. It is not, perhaps, so surprising that love's agony is so finely expressed, for this was the stock-in-trade of most serious composers around the year 1600, but few made it as convincing as Monteverdi did in that setting of 'Cruda Amarilli' which so shocked Artusi. The dissonances of the opening section immediately set the scene; the written-out ornaments in the various parts intensify the atmosphere; the *tessitura* of the soprano is extremely high, and since transpositions will embarrass the bass, it must be assumed that such vocal strain is part of Monteverdi's emotional plan. Then there is the jerkiness in tempo, slow passages suddenly interrupted by fast ones in an unconventional way. Guarini's puppet shepherds had rarely felt so genuinely neurotic before, and the settings by people like Marenzio and Pallavicino seem quite restrained at the side of this overwrought music. 'Ah dolente partita' shows that this is no flash in the pan. The agony is much the same, and the conclusion, with its constant dissonance, is very fine. There is an equal tautness in 'Voi pur da me partite', the tensions created by eccentric melodic patterns and the seemingly endless repetition of the phrase 'E separarsi e non sentir dolore' (And to part and not to feel pain), for which Monteverdi has invented the brilliant image of two voices starting on a unison and separating themselves slowly and dissonantly, to bring about a splendidly expressive climax.

Neurosis is not difficult to express in such an idiom. It is harder to provide music which is more playful while remaining essentially serious, but this is what Monteverdi does with the greatest assurance in such pieces as 'A un giro sol de' bell' occhi lucenti' and 'Ohimè, se tanto amate di sentir dir ohimè'. The latter is a setting of a typical erotic verse of Guarini. There is little emotional involvement in the text, for it is the working out of a poetic conceit, the attempt to make the lover seem to sigh a thousand times. Monteverdi provides an exact counterpart. He takes a conventional 'sigh' motive, a falling third in the melody usually preceded by a rest, and constructs the whole madrigal from it. Sometimes it is a consonant sigh, sometimes dissonant; sometimes it confirms the tonality of the piece, sometimes it provides a curious bitonal effect. The concentration on this motive even excludes the conventional final cadence, and since such words as 'moro' (I die) and 'languido e doloroso' (drooping and grieving) are strictly subordinated to the sighs, we know exactly what these portentous sentiments are worth. It is a perfect example of mannerist artificiality, a detail distorting the whole conception, an intellectual conceit taking charge of the music's emotional development. It is the music of flirtation, meant to appeal to anyone who enjoys such amorous sport. 'A un giro sol de' bell' occhi lucenti' is not very different. The poem is not unlike that of 'Ecco mormorar l'onde' of *Book Two*. The first section of it is descriptive, full of external imagery. The eyes of the beloved turn, and the very air around them seems to smile; the sea is calmed, the winds are quietened, the sky is adorned with another star. Then comes the contrast. Only the lover is left to weep in his unsatisfied state; from her cruelty is born his death. The music of the opening is not very far from that of Monteverdi's earlier style. The turning eyes produce a 'turn' in the melody, the smile appears on the singer's lips, made by an appropriate melisma; the calm sea only slightly undulates the common major chord, and the winds begin with a swift canon but are quickly resolved in a descending phrase. But when the first person enters the verse, the musician's agony appears with it. There is an abrupt chromatic change. Dissonance follows dissonance, and the soothing phrase of the death-wish is deliberately awkward for the singer. This is not perhaps unexpected. What is new is the scale on which the intensity is created. In 'Ecco mormorar l'onde' the more personal note was struck only briefly at the end of a large madrigal. Here it takes up well over a third of the whole and dominates the piece. Feeling, not observation, is the aim this time.

'A un giro sol de' bell' occhi lucenti' strikes this deeper vein in

Monteverdi, but because of its pictorialism keeps the eroticism in decent bounds; which is more than can be said of 'Si ch'io vorrei morire'. The poet again works out the double meaning of the word 'death'. 'I wish to die', he begins, 'now I feel the lovely mouth of my beloved'. He enlarges on the kisses. First he is content with a love-bite – and indeed no wonder, for 'In this sweetness of her breast I am extinguished'. He hurries to the climax, tasting the lips, in a conventional kiss, then biting voluptuously again – and then he 'dies'. In itself it is not a distinguished poem; but Monteverdi is ready to seek out its potentialities. The wish to die is repeated three times in a meaningful descent. The mouth of the beloved arouses him again. He bites with a delicious dissonance; as it is about to resolve, the discord bites again, and again, and yet again. But the rising phrase is extinguished in conventionally falling suspensions until the cadence settles in the bottom register of the voices. He calls for haste in a canon, so hasty that there is but a single crotchet between the parts.

Ex. 9

She playfully resists. He tries once more, using three voices so that two of them continually push the third up and up. She shows less resistance this time (using three voices instead of five, as before), but now nothing can hold him back. The canon resumes in the sopranos, the bass pleads 'Ah mouth, ah kisses, ah tongue'. He conquers – and 'dies' with the very first descending phrase. The composer who can do this understands love; and these shepherds are no idealised rustics. They are very human.

There are several madrigals of this power – 'Era l'anima mia già presso a l'ultim' hore' is especially fine – and the erotic world they create is so strong that we may be tempted to think that it is not far to that of *L'Incoronazione di Poppea*. But the opera is nearly forty years off, and there is one massive problem yet to be solved. An opera requires a stamina not always granted to a composer of songs, and elsewhere in these madrigal books Monteverdi shows that he has not so far acquired it. There are two madrigal cycles in the *First Book*: 'Ecco Silvio' in five sections, and 'Ch'io t'ami', a more modest venture in three.

The linked series of madrigals had become very popular in the years around the turn of the century. This attempt to transcend the miniature nature of the genre met with varying success. The most promising way of creating a large form was probably to provide a background story from which a great variety of moods could arise, and such so-called 'madrigal comedies' as Vecchi's *L'Amfiparnaso* or Banchieri's *Il festino nella sera del giovedì grasso avanti cena* are most entertaining. The more serious madrigal cycles, on the other hand, generally set a poem of some length and have a greater obstacle to overcome, in the narrow range of emotions embodied in the verse. Marenzio's two extended cycles, 'Giovane Donna', a setting of Petrarch, and 'Se quel dolor' (by Trojano) published in his *Sixth Book of Madrigals* in 1595, both suffer from this tendency to monotony to some extent, although the form is certainly interesting in its combination of varying textures. The basic trouble with such works is that they use an advanced idiom essentially conceived to express a small lyrical idea, and nothing is more wearying than continuous emotionalism. In 'Ecco Silvio', Monteverdi seems determined to avoid this at any cost. It is a Wertian, recitative-like piece, with long stretches of uneventful homophony. There are some harmonic asperities for the occasional evocative word, not to mention some mild ornamentations for 'sospiri' (sighs) and a sudden chromatic change to set 'Ah garzon crudo, ah cor senza pietà (Ah, cruel boy, ah, heart without mercy). But on the whole it seems to have lost subtlety of texture, for Monteverdi's best music has so far always had some contrapuntal passages, and merely transferring the melody from one group of voices to another is too ingenuous a procedure for such an extended work. 'Ch'io t'ami' is much more effective. Its basis is still the choral recitative, but it remains only a basis. 'Di quest' alpestri monti' (Of those wild mountains) produces a series of leaps, a couple of them of a tenth, which immediately add life. The climax of the cycle, at the beginning of the last number, has some real Monteverdian dissonance, the following recitative only acting as a brief interruption before a powerful chromatic passage brings back the atmosphere. The cycle does not, perhaps, have the sheer intensity that is the achievement of some of the single madrigals. Still, it is much more effective than the trilogy of *Book Three*, and suggests that the composer was increasing his ambitions and developing a taste for the large scale.

This is exactly what he required in the next few years. Two years after the *Fifth Book* was published (and that it was a huge success with the public is certain from the number of reprints it achieved), the production of Monteverdi's first opera *L'Orfeo* took place. This too was a success. Given first to an 'academy', a society of intellectuals, it was repeated shortly afterwards before the assembled nobility of Mantua and surrounding courts. It was eventually published, an uncommon honour for an opera at this time, and then reprinted in 1615 – something quite unheard of. Its success was due very largely to Monteverdi's experience as a madrigalist. In the First Act he wrote a fine series of canzonets, in the Second a huge madrigalian lament and for the Third he composed a big *scena* in which Orpheus persuades the boatman to ferry him across to Hades to rescue his beloved Euridice. And it was this last piece which gave him the idea for a philosophy of opera. In each one he was to write a central set-piece, to act as the focal point of the drama. In the next opera, *L'Arianna*, it was a lament of the heroine, and from accounts of the first performance it is clear that it was this that caused the furore. The *scena* became what can only be called a 'hit', for its popularity went far beyond the normal confines of the noble audience. It was printed in various arrangements, imitated by scores of lesser composers, and set a vogue which persisted in various forms until the eighteenth century.

The 'Lament of Ariadne', of course, fitted in well with the mannerist gloom of its time. It was the logical result of the settings of the pastoral laments from Guarini's *Il Pastor Fido* and the fashionable Counter-Reformation poem *Gerusalemme liberata* of Tasso, with its battlefield deaths (the scene is set on a crusade). Nevertheless the sheer power of Monteverdi's piece must surely derive from the personal tragedy which had recently beset him. His wife had died. Monteverdi had retired to seek solace and the aid of his father at Cremona, but he had not been allowed to rest there in peace. He had been called back to Mantua to compose *L'Arianna* for a festival of opera arranged to celebrate the wedding of the Duke's son. It had taken every bit of his various friends' powers of persuasion to get him to go, and he nearly killed himself with a vast year's work when he finally went back. Nor were his troubles at an end. During the preparations for *L'Arianna* the prima donna Caterina Martinelli died. She was a girl still in her teens and had been found some time before by the Mantuan Resident in Rome as a possible future virtuoso. She had lived in Monteverdi's house – his wife, herself a singer, could have been her teacher. He felt her loss very deeply. At the end of the festival he retired again to Cremona and now it was even more difficult to make him return to the Mantua which he actively hated. His early forties were the nadir of Monteverdi's life.

The *Sixth Book of Madrigals* came out after he had finally left Mantua, but its contents are for the most part – perhaps even entirely – the work of his last five years there. As we might expect, they show his depression, and this time it is no fashionable gloom, but an intensely personal

expression of emotion. Nearly half the book is taken up with two
madrigal cycles, one an arrangement of the 'Lament of Ariadne', the
other a 'Sestina' on the death of Caterina Martinelli. The natural
seriousness of these is reflected in the single madrigals too, 'Misero
Alceo' and 'Batto qui pianse Ergasto' are in much the same vein, and
even a more cheerful piece such as 'Zefiro torna e'l bel tempo rimena'
makes the most of such lines as:

> But with mee wretch the storms of w
> & heavy sighs, which from my heart
> That took the kay thereof to heaven fc
> So that singing of byrds & spring tim
> & ladies love that mens affection gaine
> Are like a desert, & cruell beastes devo

to quote a contemporary translation. The two cycles
magnificent madrigalian works ever written. The *sc*
admittedly retains the flavour of solo melody in one
Monteverdi has obviously reworked the material a
some ways made it stronger than in the existing mor
actual original form it took in the opera has been
opening with its immediate clashes between the upp
bass must gain with the sustained harmonies of voic
harpsichord or any other keyboard accompaniment;
teverdi lengthens various parts and elaborates the for
section, by repeating the opening twice, the second tim
in the middle with an impassioned outcry 'and who wo
comfort me, with my cruel fate . . .'. Who indeed
Monteverdi in 1608?

But if this 'Lament' is fine, the 'Sestina' is still more re
verse is frankly bad. It is mannerist pastoralism at its
conceits, without any real depth of feeling in its descr
shepherd at the tomb of his beloved. It has no real solid in
this reason might seem to present difficulties to the comp
other hand, it has a plethora of emotional words: 'ala
'torment', 'wounds' – this is its essence. Monteverdi found
fitted his mood very well. His basic musical idea was t
recitative-madrigal style, as in 'Dorinda, ah dirò mia, se n
from the previous book. But an immense change has com
style. There are, it is true, a few neutral moments in
manner, as at the beginning of the third section 'Darà la

THE ROYAL EXCHANGE LONDON

Royal Exchange
Assurance
INCORPORATED
1720

HEAD OFFICE
ROYAL EXCHANGE
LONDON, E.C. 3.

39

where consonant harmony and declamatory melody provide a brief interlude from the passion which surrounds it; and some parts of 'Ma te raccoglie, o Ninfa' are similarly restrained. Far more typical is the very beginning of the cycle, 'Incenerite spoglie, avara tomba'. The tenor begins the recitative most innocently, it is taken up by the other voices equally so. Then in the fifth bar the minor chord is changed to the major and a rich modulation to another key takes place. This is no artless recitative, but one in which a wide range of harmonic device is at the composer's disposal. Moreover, the recitative is soon broken by the lover's cries 'ahi lasso', the first of the madrigalian symbols which constantly recur throughout the piece. For Monteverdi applies the technique of his most sophisticated madrigals (such as 'Si ch'io vorrei morire') to the larger form. The man who could convey the fluctuating intensities of the art of love now uses the same means in, for example, 'Ditelo, o fiumi e voi ch'udiste' to convey the fluctuating depth of misery of the bereaved man. He begins with the major key as Glaucon contemplates the pastoral stream; he adds force by making the *tutti* repeat his crying, bar after bar. Then he shows the true pathos of the situation in a duet full of dissonance and the minor key. There is a moment of comfort by the full ensemble, but the duet comes back exactly as before, insisting on Glaucon's grief. The ensemble tries again, this time with very soothing consonances, but it is no good. The duet returns as before, and now the ensemble can only join in; and as it amplifies the duet, the dissonances are amplified too, made richer and more tragic by the sheer weight of five-part harmony. This is the kind of thing which happens continually throughout the six madrigals. It is very far from the eccentricities of Wert or Monteverdi's own earlier works in this style. Perhaps even more significant is the control of the total effect of the cycle. In the 'Lament of Ariadne' he makes certain of the unity of the cycle by using thematic links between the various numbers – not in an obvious way but, it must be said, not particularly magically either. In the 'Sestina' there is no need for this. Monteverdi shows a natural flair for building up different levels of climax. The first section has only a short period of dissonant anguish, the second extends this, but the dissonance, on the whole, is kinder. The third begins to build up the tension, to reach an eventual enormous climax at the beginning of the fifth section, where discord follows vicious discord, while the upper voices provide broken cries of 'ohimè'. It is not yet all over. The final section, having started in quiet recitative, suddenly seems to be about to relieve the gloom as the name 'Corinna' echoes throughout the pastoral landscape, to a conventional canzonetta motive (much used by even the lighter English madrigalists), so that the shepherdess comes back to life for a moment. It is in vain; she is dead and Glaucon's cries go on and on, becoming more and more shrill, until he falls back completely exhausted. This section has an indescribable physical effect on the nerves, the repeated short phrases (and they are no more than short rhythmic tags) battering on both listener's consciousness and singer's voice until both must feel as overwrought as did Monteverdi himself in his year of agony. There is nothing quite like this anywhere in the madrigalian literature. If Gesualdo provided at times as neurotic a music, his works are brief; this 'Sestina' is sustained and wearying. It was the end of the road for the mannerist madrigal. Nothing more could be said in this idiom.

Concerto in Venice

It was nearly the end of the road for Monteverdi as well. His father, writing to Mantua in 1608, was quite certain that any more work and he would be dead. But the thin, wiry figure which stares out of the portraits indicates a native North Italian toughness. His creative life was not yet half over when he wrote the 'Sestina'. On the other hand, he clearly could not go on living on his nerves indefinitely, and in a way it must have been a relief to have a change of direction forced on him when in 1612, after twenty years' service in Mantua, he was unceremoniously dismissed by the Duke. The reason for the break is not known but it seems likely that Monteverdi refused to write music for a festive occasion on the usual short notice given by his employer. 'Presto et bene, insieme non conviene', he probably said, this time once too often. Still, it was a blessing in disguise. He had the chance of a year's rest in Cremona at his father's house (they were obviously a long-living family). Then he was awarded the fruits of his genius. He was appointed *maestro di cappella* at St Mark's, Venice, a well-paid, agreeable post in which he felt (justly) appreciated, and was to live contentedly for the next thirty years. For Monteverdi the madrigal composer this meant a completely new outlook. Whereas at Mantua the madrigal was an essential ingredient of the concert life of which he had been in charge, in Venice it was no more than a side-line for him. There were concerts and 'academies' in the Serene Republic, and Monteverdi was pleased enough to accept fees for arranging the music and composing for them, but his main job was to provide large-scale church music for Doge and Senate. When he did make a major effort in secular music, it was to be in the field of opera and other dramatic entertainments for foreign courts. There were to be no large madrigal cycles, no 'sestinas', and there were to be only two large books of secular music in his Venetian period, aside from a smaller volume of songs collected by his publisher and some pieces printed in anthologies. This works out at no more than three or four pieces each year, many of them quite short. Clearly his main energies went elsewhere.

There is perhaps another reason for the change. By the time the *Sixth Book of Madrigals* was published in 1614, the classic five-part madrigal was already out of date. A few old-fashioned composers in the provinces went on using the genre; the moderns had already turned to music in the

42

concerted style. The main vehicle for these was the solo song, the voice accompanied by harpsichord or lute (and sometimes the Spanish guitar), whose relatively subordinate role was made obvious by its notation. For whereas the singer's part was written out in full, the accompanist was given merely the bass and some figures underneath it to indicate the harmonies to be used. There were various forms of songs which the composer could use. There was the madrigal, as it was still called, the main feature of which was the word-painting, often suggested by verse of the Guarini style. The words were held to be enough to shape such pieces, as indeed they were in the music in the *stile rappresentativo*, in which the poem was 'declaimed' rather than sung, in a serious (but vain) attempt to recreate the essence of ancient Greek music. Then there were two types of 'aria', the first a simple strophic song setting words not very different from those of the sixteenth-century canzonet; the other a more complicated affair known in modern times as the 'strophic variation', in which the bass remained the same throughout several verses of the poem, while the melody was allowed to be changed to express the varied details of the words. From this sprang the use of the ostinato bass, a short melodic formula being repeated many times while variations were written over it. (The countless chaconnes and passacaglias of the seventeenth century belong to this category.)

Monteverdi was well aware of these new forms by the time he arrived in Venice. The *basso continuo* indeed had been developed in Mantua, by the organist of the cathedral, Lodovico Grossi da Viadana, and had attracted him as early as the *Fifth Book of Madrigals*, where he used it as an essential texture of the last six pieces. It was a most useful device, he had found, to make the contrasts between various vocal groupings sharper. Instead of having, say, two tenors and a bass contrasting with two sopranos and one of the tenors, it was possible just to contrast the sopranos and tenors without any loss of force, for the harmonies were continued throughout on the harpsichord. Moreover, a single voice was now a new potential colour, and the contrasts could be made more vivid still by using a florid solo part immediately followed by a more plain *tutti*. In the *Fifth Book* these lines of thought are well explored, especially in such a piece as 'Ahi, com' a un vago sol cortese giro' where Monteverdi delights in wreathed, ornamental tenor and soprano duets interrupted by a refrain which helps to organise the madrigal securely. In another, 'T'amo, mia vita', he writes a delicious flirtation song in which the soprano repeats ecstatically the lover's 'I love you, my life', while the other voices add her commentary, until they too are persuaded

to amplify the soprano phrase. But these devices are essentially develop-
ments from Monteverdi's earlier madrigals, and the atmosphere and
aims are not radically altered. Nor are they in the similarly concerted
pieces of the *Sixth Book*. In this 'Qui rise Tirsi' uses a great deal of vocal
dexterity as in the madrigals for the Three Ladies of earlier books. And
'Misero Alceo', an extremely fine (and neglected) lament, owes its depth
of emotion to the attitudes of the conventional madrigal rather than to
the use of the harpsichord, and it could be arranged in the earlier style
without much trouble. Monteverdi was not by any means always so
backward-looking – although it is significant that his most superb
music is nearly always so. His *Scherzi musicali* are accompanied duets
(they are not true trios, since the bass voice doubles the *basso continuo*) in
the manner of the strophic song. They use catchy up-to-date hemiola
rhythms and reject counterpoint almost com-
pletely. Diatonic, and built in short phrases, their tunes stick in the
memory, though when we know other composers' pieces in the same
vein, we realise that Monteverdi is not really any better at this sort of
thing than many minor figures of the time:

Ex. 10

As for the strophic variation, Monteverdi used it extensively in *L'Orfeo*,
and the ostinato technique appears in certain motets in the famous
Vespers volume of 1610, though not applied very strictly. Nevertheless,
in spite of these essays in the modern style, Monteverdi had not yet
produced a madrigal book which shows an understanding of it.

The *Seventh Book of Madrigals* came out in 1619, and a close examination hints that the truly modern manner was not much to Monteverdi's
taste. Instead of a book of popular solo madrigals and duets, such as
most composers of the time were publishing, it contains a tremendous
variety of genres with only the duets, perhaps, up-to-date, the rest
being a mixture of old and new styles. In fact the nearest model to the
volume is the work of an old rival of Monteverdi's, Marco da Gagliano,
whose book called *Musiche* appeared in 1615, and is a similar musical
rag-bag. Like Gagliano's, Monteverdi's volume contains an extended
ballet, *Tirsi e Clori*, which he had composed for the Duke of Mantua in

1615, and which was a most appropriate choice to conclude a book dedicated to the Duchess. The first number also looks as though it might have been composed as a miniature ballet of some kind. 'Tempro la cetra' is a strophic variation aria, the tenor singing four verses of a poem over a recurring bass, the verses being separated by a ritornello for five instruments. The theme of the verse is that while the lover has come to sing the praises of Mars, it is in fact Venus who benefits from his song. It is not difficult to imagine the performer dressed as a warrior, with a *corps de ballet* dancing to the formal rhythmic patterns of the ritornello; and this mode of performance becomes even more likely when, after the final verse, the instruments play an extended dance. The whole piece is closely akin to the Prologue to *L'Orfeo*, both in its technique of painting individual words with elaborate ornaments and in its general quasi-declamatory style.

Less clearly operatic are the two *lettere amorose*, or musical love-letters, written in the *stile rappresentativo*, but their deliberate dryness suggests that Monteverdi was attempting to create the type of music used by the Greeks in declaiming their dramas; and this in turn may have resulted in some sort of mimetic performance. As attempts at writing music halfway between song and speech, they are very interesting. The texts are prose, and the music is prosaic to match them. Much of the time the singer is restricted to a few middle notes in his music, departing from them only for moments of great emotion. He never repeats words, and the musical punctuation is very sensitive. The harmonic accompaniment is equally bleak, and the use of such musical devices as the repeated motive, so effectively displayed in Monteverdi's operatic recitative, is denied him. Here the philosophy is very much 'prima le parole, poi la musica' – the words first, then the music – and on paper or gramophone record these pieces seem strangely ineffective for such an essentially musical composer. Even so, in the presence of a great actor-singer they might well have been very impressive, and it is significant that these 'letters' were imitated by a number of composers immediately after Monteverdi's were published.

But these were not to be the way forward; and if this is true also of 'Con che soavità, labbra odorate' we at least should not neglect this most attractive work. It is admittedly quite difficult to assemble the resources needed. It is in a real Venetian style, using three contrasting groups of performers: one, a singer accompanied by two *chittaroni* (large lutes), a harpsichord and a spinet (or small harpsichord), the second of strings with harpsichord, the third of viola and cello (or two viols) and *contra-*

basso with an organ. This arrangement of forces, strongly influenced by the music of Andrea and Giovanni Gabrieli, admittedly cuts out all thought of exact declamation, for words must be repeated and, more important, must be given strong rhythms to keep the soprano as part of the ensemble. But the object of the piece is very different from monodic music, even though it uses a single voice: it is to show off a fascinating variety of orchestral colour, a typically Monteverdian desire. And he makes the most of it, as we can see when the lover's kisses suddenly leave him breathless – and the sound disappears to show his newly found weakness:

Ex. 11

'Con che soavità, labbra odorate' was surely written for some special occasion, an evening of chamber music at the Morosini's perhaps, or at the house of the English ambassador (Sir Thomas Wotton started a good tradition of musical patronage in the early years of the century, which continued for quite a long time), when, as Monteverdi proudly told his former employers in Mantua, 'the whole city ran to listen' to his music – which was apparently more than they had done there. It was not, however, the sort of music which sold song-books.

This was to be found in solo songs without elaborate accompaniments, or in music for small ensembles, such as duets and trios; and Monteverdi provides these latter in plenty in this *Seventh Book*. The duets are indeed amongst his greatest music, for they continue the essential themes of the later Mantuan madrigal into the new idiom. Not that the duet was so very new to Monteverdi. So much of his earlier music had contained duet and trio passages that it was merely a matter of rearranging his material to cut out the wider range of colours of the five-part madrigal. The similarities can be seen at once in 'O come sei gentile, caro augellino', a duet for sopranos which in every way reminds us of the Wertian madrigals of *Books Three* and *Four*. It is a bird song, full of pictorialism and the bright colours of the upper voices, now accentuated by the fact that solo voices could display their dexterity without interfering with the contrapuntal writing inherent in the sixteenth-century style. The ornaments are delightfully arranged so that they shape, rather than interrupt, the melodic flow, producing tuneful phrases which, since they are usually repeated by both the singers, become very memorable. Nothing quite so pleasing had been 'heard in Monteverdi's music for over twenty years, and its charm must reflect his recovery from the misery of the later Mantuan period. There are several similar pieces: 'Dice la mia bellissima Licori', a kissing song in which the technique of tossing a phrase from one voice to another conveys most appropriately the playfulness of the lovers; 'Ah, che non si conviene romper la fede?', written for two virtuoso tenors, since for the word 'lontano' (far away) Monteverdi uses two huge leaps in the manner of Wert; and 'Tornate, o cari baci', another flirtatious frivolity of the most catchy kind, with a refrain ('Baci, baci') which anyone could go on humming for days. The final masterpiece in this vein is the famous and superb 'Chiome d'oro, bel thesoro', in which two violins are added to the voices to play ritornelli and generally add to the gaiety. As usual, when Monteverdi sets himself a problem – here the use of a short and not apparently very promising ostinato bass – the results are splendid. The violin tune which appears over the top of them was so good that he used it prominently in his setting of *Beatus vir* (the Doge and Senate must have enjoyed *that* Vespers) and the soprano tune, also used in the psalm, is even more lively. Yet again we see the master at work. Most composers would have thought the provision of two such melodies enough, especially to set most trivial verse. Monteverdi goes further. He interrupts each strophe with a little cadenza for the singers. These demand skill and might be thought to be there just to show off their nimble throats; in fact, they add a touch of deeper emotion, for the harmonies which result from the dual 'improvisations' are more complex and dissonant than anything else in the song. It is a nicely judged effect.

One is glad to see Monteverdi so happy, but in fact the pick of the duets are those in which the Mantuan gloom has persisted. 'Interrotte speranze' is a very intense work, the pain of the unsatisfied lover as anguished as ever it was in *Book Four*. It begins with an obstinately held pedal note in the bass, over which the tenors, beginning on a monotone, gradually ascend the scale, eventually forcing the harmony to follow them to the foreign key (as it must be called, for it is a purely modern effect) of the dominant. If we think that the matter is going to rest there, Monteverdi immediately shows us that he is very much in earnest by going back to the beginning and doing this all over again. The technique, we may notice, is that of the old canzonet; the purpose to which it is put is anything but canzonet-like. There is a moment of relaxation as the lover hopes to persuade his mistress, but the agony returns with still more dissonance, as he thinks of her cruelty. There is little cheerfulness in this piece, and it ends with some acid harmonies, caused conventionally enough by making one tenor follow the other with the theme, the all-pervading gloom increased by the use of the lowest notes of the voices, a hollow and awe-inspiring sound. Equally Mantuan is the duet over a ground bass 'Ohimè, dov'è il mio ben?' There are four sections, each providing a new variation of the voice parts over the same bass, in this way giving a challenge to Monteverdi's technical skill. As usual, he rises to the occasion, the more so since the words belong to the kind which had inspired his laments in his last madrigal book. To quote a few lines of Bernardo Tasso's poem in Thomas Watson's paraphrase of 1590:

> Alas where is my love, where is my sweeting
> That hath stolen my heart, God send us meeting
> That ruing my lament with friendly greeting
> She may release my smart and all my weeping.

Having only two voices and harpsichord made most of the composers of the early seventeenth century more clear-cut in their harmony, more innocent in the emotional life of their music. Monteverdi, if anything, seems to be able to find in the medium just as rich possibilities as in the five-part madrigal, as his opening phrases make clear (Ex. 12).

It is not just his harmony either which makes the work so expressive. His contrapuntal skill comes in, in an unlikely way. There is little pure doubling of the voices; nearly always they are at odds with one another, now prodding each other by dissonance, now amplifying each other's phrases, now shortening them by interruptions which at the climaxes

Ex. 12

may be abrupt and powerful. And if this is the technique of the composer skilled in sixteenth-century music, the gift of melody shows that Monteverdi is very much a modern. The ornamental lines follow the meaning of the verbal detail as closely as anyone could desire, elaborating the word 'lievi' (trifling) or the exclamation 'ahi' (alas). Indeed the ornaments do much more; they make the melody grow, balancing the phrases, giving emphasis where it is needed, and in general fulfilling a musical function. This is very accomplished music.

In spite of the intensity in these duets, in his *Seventh Book of Madrigals* one can sense the change in Monteverdi. Such passion is rare; a more detached attitude is taking its place. This was partly a general change. After the violence of the turn of the century music had become more pleasing and more innocent. Monteverdi's young men at St Mark's were among the leading song-writers of the day, and Alessandro Grandi, Giambattista Berti and, later, Francesco Cavalli were turning to more popular styles. Not for them the philosophic problems so essential to their immediate forebears, with their endless discussions on what the Greeks really meant. Not for them, either, the idea that the words should dictate the musical shapes and manners. Music was becoming more pure, returning to its basic independence of the pre-madrigalian era. If the medium to be used was song, or duet, it was the attractiveness of the tune which mattered, not how closely it expressed the words; if the Vesper psalms were to be set, it was the shape of the music which controlled the way it was to be done, even if it meant altering the order of the words (Monteverdi was a great one for inserting refrains, words and all); in opera, it was soon to be the aria – a *musical* form – which dominated the drama. Alongside this tendency in technique there seems to go a fundamental turning away from high seriousness in spirit. Perhaps madrigalian music had always been dominated by the writers of the canzonettas, but as well as a huge bulk of light music there had always been giants attempting to 'move the whole man'. When the generation born in the latter part of the sixteenth century had gone, no great composers took their place – at least in secular music (although Counter-Reformation Rome gave us the religious works of Carissimi). Monteverdi could hardly escape the effect of this trend. In the music he published in the anthologies of the 1620s and in the collection of *Scherzi musicali*, which his publisher Bartholomeo Magni put together in 1632, there is a new note of frivolity. The results are pleasant enough, but Monteverdi is not particularly good at it. His purely strophic songs such as 'Maledetto sia l'aspetto' and 'La mia turca che d'amor' have well-turned tunes, but these have a tendency to outstay their welcome when all the verses are sung. As usual the technical challenge of the strophic variation stimulates him more, and 'Ohimè ch'io cado, ohimè ch'inciampo' manages to depict quite a number of the verbal images without any disturbance of its walking bass. So does 'Quel sguardo sdegnosetto', a splendid song, with its three verses bound together by an appealing refrain which gives variety with a range of harmonic resource all the more impressive because it is not in any way outrageous. A C major tonality can easily seem to drift into A minor if the melody begins a couple of beats later, and a note held back a little becomes a most effective dissonance to contrast with the predominantly firm consonance. Such means are those of Purcell and Bach, and Monteverdi surely belongs to this company in his treatment of recurring bass parts.

This liking for the strophic variation, of course, is the result of Monteverdi's concern with verbal expression, which continued, in spite of the change of musical climate, until the end of his life. His letters indeed show us that he was thinking more intensively than ever about it. He was especially concerned with the Platonic ideas of 'imitation'. The concept was capable of two divergent interpretations (not to mention a host of variations in emphasis). Man's emotions can be 'imitated' in music; and the sounds of everyday life can be introduced into music. These two ideas are not mutually exclusive, and in poetry the image is so much part of the technique of expressing emotions that they may coincide. For the composer it is not quite as easy. The sounds of life are not so capable of emotional overtones as verbal images, and those which are may still not be the stuff of highly organised music.

Monteverdi saw the dichotomy, and his letters indicate that he wavered between the two views. In those concerning the lost opera called *Licori, la finta pazza* he was very tempted by the chance to convey the rapid changes in mood which are so much a part of any human being, and by choosing a lover who pretends to be mad, as his heroine, he wanted to accentuate these changes. He insists that his prima donna must base her acting

> . . . on the meaning of the word rather than of the phrase, so that when she speaks of war she must imitate war, when of peace, peace, and when of death, she must convey the idea of death, and so on. And because the transformations take place in the shortest space of time, so must the imitation . . .[1]

At the same time realism was becoming increasingly important to him. His dramatic *scena*, *Il Combattimento di Tancredi e Clorinda*, first produced in the Mocenigo palace in 1624, is a battle piece in which the imitation is of the most obvious and deliberate kind, such effects as 'Trotting of the Horse', 'the clashing of swords' and so on being marked as such in the score. And it is this dual approach to the problems of composition which gave fruit in the *Eighth Book of Madrigals*, subtitled *Madrigals of War and Love*. His explanation of his aims is given in a lengthy foreword to the volume[2], and leans heavily on Plato for support of their somewhat eccentric working out. His basic idea is that there are three 'humours' in man (this came from contemporary medical theory): stillness, agitation, and supplication. These correspond to the states of calmness, war, and love or passion; and music (following Plato again) must be able to inspire these in its listeners. Since other composers have been concerned with calmness and love, leaving aside war, Monteverdi proposes to show how an 'agitated' style can be used. This *stile concitato*, as he called it, involves the use of certain rhythms suggested by Plato, and his battle music follows these quite strictly.

As we read through this foreword, it may seem an extraordinarily muddled document for an intensely practical composer to write, until we realise that such theorising is not uncommon when an artist is in need of renewal. Wagner and Stravinsky, to seek no further, both did something similar after exhausting the manner inherited from their

1 His letter of 7 May 1627, quoted in G. F. Malipiero, *Monteverdi* (Milan, 1929), p. 252.
2 An English translation is given in full in O. Strunk, *Source Readings in Music History* (London, 1952), pp. 413–15.

predecessors. It requires no psychologist to see that Monteverdi's youthful ardour has given out, and must be replaced by another, more detached attitude; and also that, since he cannot accept the frivolous style of his younger contemporaries, he must justify, to himself and his audience, a continuation of his 'academic' seriousness. The coolness coming on him can be seen if we compare such a work as 'O come vaghi, o come cari', published in an anthology in 1624, with the chaconne 'Zefiro torna', included in the *Scherzi musicali* in 1632. 'O come vaghi, o come cari' is the duet equivalent of 'A un giro sol de' bell' occhi lucenti' of *Book Four*, beginning with the same kind of opening section which is on the whole descriptive and slightly detached. The rays of Lydia's eyes are suggested by the straight, scalewise phrases, Cupid's darts by an extremely vivid phrase, in which the very declamation of the word 'dardetti' with its deliberate misaccentuation seems to be the exact equivalent of the shooting of the arrows, and the division of the motive between the voices powerfully sets the scene.

Ex. 13

Yet there is the old Monteverdi still at work, for just as in 'A un giro sol de' bell' occhi lucenti' the pictorial first section was only there to make the lover's pain seem more anguished, so here love's wounds are made greater by the turning of the barbed dissonances at each possible cadential resting point. And again, as in the earlier piece, the proportions are such that the weight lies on the lover's personal feelings, not on the descriptive elements which set the scene. This is exactly the reverse of 'Zefiro torna'; it is the equivalent of 'Ecco mormorar l'onde' of his Cremona days. It is more technically accomplished, certainly. Its ostinato bass is a two-bar pattern which apparently allows for very little variety. The problem is to create an extended piece (for the poem is a long sonnet, not a short lyric) without monotony of either phrase-length or harmony. Monteverdi's solution is so fine as almost to defy description. The phrase-lengths of the bass are so skilfully disguised that we hardly notice them. Two-bar, four-bar, single-bar patterns are created by overlapping the voices, sharing the material between them in new ways. As for the harmony, the basic chords are used page after page, but passing notes create infinite variety, and by treating a single note in the second bar of the ostinato bass now as unessential, now as the root of a separate chord, the harmonic rhythm is given new interest. It is all very simple, all very effective. Over the top of the bass, the tenors sing a melody which always finds a musical image for the rich imagery of the verse. The zephyrs, the sweet sounds of the waves, the rustling of the leaves, the dancing in the fields, the echoes on the valleys and the mountains, nothing is missed. As the thoughts of the lover lead to self-pity, for only he is alone in this spring landscape, Monteverdi even breaks the chaconne and interposes a recitative passage with suitably doleful harmonies, complete with a chromatic groan of a most startling kind, at least in this context.

Ex. 14

This sudden startling change is very revealing, for we suddenly realise that in Monteverdi's more passionate music this would have been not nearly so unusual. But this piece is concerned more with the scene than with the agony of the shepherds. The proportions are the opposite of 'O come vaghi, o come cari'; we are back to the spirit of the 1580s.

There are indeed many similarities. The sort of poetry Monteverdi chooses in the last twenty years of his life is the Tasso kind – much of it by Guarini in his playful, not erotic manner. The tortuous double meanings of Marini and other baroque poets have gone. We are back to pastoral spring, with elegant rather than earthy shepherds and shepherdesses. The delight in vocal virtuosity has returned. 'Mentre vaga Angioletta' need only replace its tenor by soprano clefs and we would be in the world of the Ferrarese Ladies again, though it must be said that they would have to have improved even their dexterity to match these Venetian tenors. Above all the charm is back, made easier if anything by the techniques of the duet and monody. The dialogue 'Bel Pastor dal cui bel guardo' has as its essence the flirtation, effortlessly carried on by alternating duple time for the serious moments and smooth triple time, complete with teasing hemiola cadences, for the less profound emotions. Love's war ('skirmishing' might be a better word for it) provokes some fanfare motives in 'Armato il cor d'adamantina fede', but if the issue is in doubt in the middle of the piece, with its contrapuntal interplay between the two voices, victory is clearly indicated in their unanimity in the closing section. The lovers dance in 'Alle danze', yet there is nothing in the least sensuous about their strongly rhythmic trio (they are surely in restraining company). The shepherds have a similarly lively dance in 'Su su, Pastorelli vezzosi', a canzonet which, even to its suggestion of learnedness in its second part, is very like those of his Cremona days, and which forgets that the harpsichord is there to be used on its own account, merely allowing it to double the voices.

The pick of these charming pieces, however, are perhaps the works *alla francese* – in the French style – a term the meaning of which is not quite clear, but seemingly refers to somewhat evenly measured rhythms and the alternation of solo and *tutti*. 'Dolcissimo uscignolo' in this manner will always remain a great favourite of madrigal ensembles, for its simplicity hides an art rarely equalled in frankly tuneful music. The poem, by Guarini, is the one of which a paraphrase was set by Orlando Gibbons as 'Dainty fine bird' – and the Englishman typically is more melancholic as he amplifies his concluding 'Thou liv'st singing, but I sing and die', with suspensions and pedal notes. Monteverdi is merely wistful. He varies his phrase-lengths, and provides a number of different endings for the phrase 'O felice augelletto' (O happy bird). His cadences are varied also, a false relation now conveying doubt when the major key seems too forthright, a minor key now suggesting that the lover must remain resigned to his fate. All these works use pictorialism:

'Dolcissimo uscignolo' deliberately to paint the bird singing; 'Mentre vaga Angioletta' extravagantly, so that every word appears to merit interpretation, from the *roulades* for expressing 'veloce' (speedily) to the broken melody to convey the heavy breathing of 'respir' (breathes); others somewhere in between these two extremes. As long as the object remains charm, the style works very well. Where, on the other hand, the music becomes more ambitious, its limitations become apparent. The big war-like pieces such as 'Altri canti di Marte' and 'Altri canti d'amor' and 'Ardo, avvampo mi struggo' show their weaknesses. The picture conveyed is vivid enough: there are always strong rhythms to suggest the marching armies, trumpet fanfares to urge them to battle; rapid scale passages, often resulting in frightful, though always hasty, harmonic clashes, convey the confusions of the battle. The only thing is that after a little time the ear longs for something more sophisticated. The fanfares are the stuff of military music, and perhaps to an old stager like Monteverdi, who had never forgotten his journeys to the wars in Hungary in 1595, it had the fascination of reminiscence. But nothing is so tiresome as other men's campaigns; and perhaps the best that can be said is that these battle pieces are not quite as dull as Jannequin's 'La Bataille de Marignan', another 'gimmicky' piece which had the same vogue in the sixteenth century that Monteverdi's *stile concitato* had in the seventeenth.

From his descriptive music we might deduce that Monteverdi had lost his gift for powerful emotional expression. This would be quite wrong. There are some other pieces which show that this genius remained with him to the end. Significantly, though, they are works which return to the favourite themes of his Mantuan years, and most especially to that obsession with loneliness that after the death of his wife had resulted in the 'Lament of Ariadne'. One particularly fine piece to work out this deeply felt theme is the duet 'O sia tranquillo il mare'. Whether the sea is calm or rough, says the poet, he will remain waiting for his love to return. There is no sign of his Phillida, and his laments are carried away on the winds. In retrospect, it seems almost a study for *Il Ritorno d'Ulisse*, for it uses the same techniques as we find there, with a division between quasi-recitative and smoothly flowing triple time in a kind of duet aria. Monteverdi begins by painting the scene. The duet begins on a single chord as the sea's stillness demands, but after half a dozen bars the voices rise. 'Never, never', they repeat, 'shall I leave here'. The passionate dissonances, the upper registers of the tenors convey the despair.

Ex. 15

This is no purely descriptive piece; as he waits, the lover's expectations are disappointed in the irregular phrase-lengths by which one singer replies to another. The motives are short and never develop to form a long breathing melody; the discords are never far away; the minor key is stressed continuously. Then, as though he could bear to contain his anguish no longer, he bursts into the aria 'You, you never return'. It takes two or three short agonised phrases before the music flows freely, and then it repeats the words endlessly, tossing them from one voice to the other, one interrupting the other, before both unite in their complaint. Phillida does not hear. The triple time gives way to a slower passage which gradually sinks to the cadence, with a final unison. Phillida – or should it be Claudia Monteverdi? – will never return.

There is description in the music of this duet, but the proportions are right. It is personal emotion that is its *raison d'être*, not the external situation. And this is true on a much larger scale in the setting of Petrarch's sonnet 'Hor che 'l ciel e la terra'. Monteverdi puts this amongst the madrigals of war; it really belongs to those of love. It is true that the lover feels in a warlike state, as he contemplates his lack of fortune in love, and it is equally true that Monteverdi misses no opportunity to write his battle music. Nor can the piece be divorced from his Platonic theories which seem to us so muddled. It is a perfect demonstration of the three 'humours' or states of mind. It begins on a single sustained chord with the state of calm, for the picture Petrarch paints is of a still night, with heaven and earth completely silent. But the lover is in agony and the voices soar quite suddenly into a state of supplication, dissonances, Wertian melodic asperities speaking of his pain. Then he determines to win the battle in the mind: fanfares and military rhythms naturally ensue. Here they seem in place. Monteverdi is trying to convey an emotional pattern, to show the rapid changes of mood as essentially part of the psychology of love. His madrigal hinges on the meaning of the word, in the way he demanded of his singer in the lost opera *Licori finta pazza*, and war is simply an incidental idea.

There is also a kind of pictorialism in the finest of his late madrigals, the 'Lament of the Nymph', although it is certainly more clearly a psychological work than either 'Hor che 'l ciel e la terra' or 'O sia tranquillo il mare'. Three men set a familiar scene:

> Phoebus had not yet given the new day to the world, when a young maiden came from her house. Her pallid face showed her sorrow, and her sighs often came from the depth of her heart. She lamented her lost love, and walked around unthinkingly, treading on the flowers.

Monteverdi's music at first sight is not so familiar. It is not cold; neither is it fully expressive. There are a few discords to show his sympathy for the maiden, but the music is really choral recitative. It is only an introduction to her song:

> 'Love', she said, stopping to regard the sky, 'Love, where is the faithfulness which the traitor swore to me? Make him return my love for him or kill me, so that I may no longer suffer such torments.'

This is a song for a soprano, and Monteverdi realises that its full strength requires his usual tautness of technique. He sets it as an ostinato, the bass endlessly repeating a short laconic figure:

Ex. 16

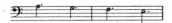

The maiden sings a most marvellous melody. At times it wrings the heart with long phrases which tax the breath and capacity for smooth singing. At other times, the pain of her loneliness demands a broken, sighing line, full of strange melodic turns. Always the bass continues, now relaxing the maiden's plea with consonance, now contradicting her melody and producing anguished dissonance of a most vicious kind. This is Monteverdi's greatest lament – and by this melody alone he 'moved the whole man' to pity. But he has not left it with just this melody. The three men join in the song: 'Ah, miserable maiden', they cry, 'she cannot suffer his coldness'. These are words of description. They provide an objectivity against which the emotions of the girl grow and overwhelm us. Monteverdi's instructions for the performers increase this contrast between feeling and detachedness. The girl is to sing freely, using *tempo rubato* as is needed to express her emotions. The men, on the other hand, must sing strictly in time. And meanwhile the bass goes on and on; the maiden will never see her love requited. Her voice dies away. Only the men are left.

So her voice is raised to the sky, amid her angry weeping. Love often puts fire in the heart of one lover, ice in the heart of the other.

Monteverdi's epilogue is even more non-committal than his prologue. The case is hopeless, there is nothing more for us to do.

In his last operas Monteverdi used all the resources of the stage to gain a picture of life which is intensely real and astonishingly comprehensive. There are few aspects of personality which are not illuminated in *L'Incoronazione di Poppea*, few operas in which the atmosphere is more vividly defined. Was Nero a portrait from life of Vincenzo Gonzaga, we may wonder? He was, as we know, quite capable of putting to death any Senecas who impeded his path. Was Poppea really Vincenzo's mistress Agnese d'Argotti? Be this as it may, it is absolutely certain that without the madrigals such works could not have been written. The laments of Octavia and Otho, the flirtations of the *valletto* and his maiden, the eroticism of Poppea herself, have all been seen in the great madrigal books. And, in a way, they are more accessible there than in the opera. Putting all operas on the stage is fraught with hazards, and Monteverdi's most of all, since we know so little of their orchestration, the style of their *mis-en-scène*, and we still find their conventions foreign to us. But for the madrigals we need no more than a few singers, a harpsichord and, at times, a few string players. The singers must be skilled, although not as a rule excessively so. Then this perfect observation of human character and experience is ours. We are the equals of the Gonzagas, the Mocenigos, and the Farnesi. Their courts have faded away. Our rich heritage remains, for he was truly

Il divino Claudio.

Index